SO YOU SAID YES

The Weiser Way to Network Marketing

by Donna J. Weiser

SO YOU SAID YES

The Weiser Way to Network Marketing

by Donna J. Weiser

Published by Weiser Publishing Company

First published 2023 Manufactured in the United States
ISBN 979-8-218-18130-7

Library of Congress CIP data applied for.

Notice: The information in this book is true and complete to the best of our knowledge. It is offered without guarantee on the part of the author or Weiser Publishing Company. The author disclaims all liability in connection with the use of this book.

Printed in the USA

DEDICATION

This book is dedicated to my beautiful mother, Shirley Olshansky (may she rest in peace) who supported me from the very first day I said “yes” to my Network Marketing business. She was my best customer and greatest cheerleader.

FOREWORD

The journey of succeeding in Network Marketing is both immensely challenging and rewarding. Once you decide and say "Yes" to the adventure, you won't want to waste any time rethinking your decision. You said "yes" and, trust me, you are in the right place!

Wisdom is the ability to discern what is true, right, and lasting. Donna Weiser is a wise woman. In her book, *So, You Said Yes!*, she has laid down the sure steppingstones to make your Network Marketing journey efficient, fun and richly rewarding.

Thirty years ago, she started what is today a massive Network Marketing business and just like you, perhaps she was a little scared and excited all at the same time.

In the beginning, she was gifted with great and loving mentors to help her launch her business. In that same way, her book will mentor you by giving you useful information and practical confidence-building action items, to help you overcome those all-too-common initial fears and find faith and ultimately success. Her book conveys her love for people and her genuine excitement over your decision to say yes to Network Marketing.

Finally, and most importantly Donna's book illustrates how one person can make a difference. She honored her own "Yes," kept her word to herself and gave to others by implementing her hope and vision to build a community of ambitious, fun-loving people.

Jump in! You're in good hands. Follow Donna's well-lit pathway for she has wisely blazed a brilliant trail. It is up to you now to go as far and as fast as you choose.

So, you have said "yes!" It's your move.

Richard Bliss Brooke

PREFACE

At the dawn of the Industrial Age, Old World farmers originally sold their foodstuffs and handcrafted goods at markets, all within a 10 mile radius. They sold their wares by walking or floating on a nearby river. With industrialization came changes to the supply and demand of rapidly expanding urban markets. Products came in great quantities and varieties as horsepower moved to engines powering trucks and railroads to deliver products to cities with greater speed and efficiency.

Product distribution, connecting products with expanding marketplaces, gave rise to a new distribution category, that of "agent," a representative presenting products and services to end users. In the New World, "pack peddlers" were agents who distributed products by carrying them on their backs to people tucked away in the mountains or along inaccessible by-ways where horses and carts could not yet go.

One such innovative peddler, a Syrian immigrant named Dawahare, quickly understood the exponential advantage of buying goods in quantity, then distributing more product through a network of peddlers. Dawahare provisioned and managed his network of agents and took a small override percentage of their sales. Dawahare knew the wisdom of maximizing distribution just as did John D. Rockefeller, who said: "I would rather earn 1% of 100 people's efforts, than 100% of my own efforts." Dawahare led his family from obscurity to prosperity, and during his lifetime, he eventually owned and operated 33 department stores in Kentucky, Tennessee and Ohio.

No matter the Age, whether personally presenting one's products or an agent acting for a producer – it is all distribution. One could say, once agents began presenting products produced by others, the field of Network Marketing was born. Thanks to the extensive research of University of Illinois at Chicago professor Dr. Charles King, Network Marketing today is a proper academic discipline for product distribution.

Fast forward to the Digital Age and changes in sales and distribution. “Click and order” is rapidly replacing “brick and mortar” as online “agents” present products across the globe via WiFi, smart devices, social media platforms and other affordable communication networks like Skype and Zoom. Predictions are that by the 2030s, 70 percent of today’s jobs will be obsolete. Taking a closer look for emerging opportunities is a good idea for many.

In my book, *So You Said Yes*, my goal is to show you how you can prosper in the ever-changing landscape of the workplace over the next 10 to 20 years. Network Marketing may possibly be a life preserver for many as a path to affordable entrepreneurship.

Over the past 30 years, I have experienced success as a Network Marketing professional, before and after the advent of the Digital Age. I understand exponential growth like Dawahare and Rockefeller experienced, and I have a clear eye focused on the opportunity global change will certainly deliver.

Donna J. Weiser

ACKNOWLEDGMENTS

This is my first book and I am so appreciative of those who have supported me on the wonderful journey.

My husband Jeff Hennes has been so supportive and encouraging since I started writing this book. He often said "So, what's happening with the book?" which always motivated me to get back to work. Thanks Honey.

I attended a fabulous leadership retreat with my mentor (and now friend), Richard Brooke. One evening we were chatting over dinner about some of my experiences, challenges and wins in my Network Marketing business when he suggested that I write a book. Thanks Richard, for planting the seed that has grown into this completed project.

When I was half way through this book, I reached out to Bruce McAllister who is an accomplished author, writing coach and former head of the creative writing program at the University of Redlands. Bruce not only encouraged me to keep writing and finish the book, he strengthened my belief in myself as a writer. Thank you Bruce.

My son-in-law, Benjamin McAllister, is a busy corporate executive and a very talented graphic artist as well. He was kind enough to take time out of his busy schedule to create the beautiful cover for my book as well as my fabulous website.

This book would never have been completed without the love and support of my dear friend and writing mentor, Eunice Ray. From the moment Eunice read my book, (before she started editing it) she was so encouraging and supportive, not only of my writing, but also of the important message to the Network Marketing community. I am so grateful to you Eunice. Thank you so much.

Donna J. Weiser

NOTE TO READER

What is Network Marketing?

In 1993, business guru Peter Drucker described the future economy as a society of networks. As we begin, I would like to briefly explain a very approachable business model built on networks.

Network Marketing is a legal and proven distribution system that companies can use to present products and/or services to the marketplace. Independent representatives may choose to work remotely to present and sell products and services directly to clients who can also duplicate their efforts by building networks or teams of distributors.

A true and lawful Network Marketing Company - not an unlawful "pyramid scheme" - has a minimal financial demand for entry, including a low sign-up fee and/or initial product order. Network Marketing's attractive low-cost entry coupled with the potential for earnings and bonuses, can reward those who also do the significant work that any meaningful endeavor requires. Too often miscalculating the significant demands of this business has caused the reputation of Network Marketing to be colored by disappointments. Many people tend to over promise and under deliver.

I invite you to read my story of decades in Network Marketing. It is my hope that through my experience, you can see the benefits of building a Network Marketing business, which include the treasured relationships gained and the personal and financial growth that have enriched my life.

Donna J. Weiser

TABLE of CONTENTS

INTRODUCTION

After 30 + years in the Network Marketing industry and having achieved the highest rank as well as being among the top 25 highest income earners in my Company, (disclaimer – I worked quite hard over the years to achieve that success) my biggest joy is to support others in creating their own success. It's my honor and privilege to share some thoughts, wisdom, tips and suggestions, so that you might benefit from my many years as a Network Marketing Professional.

Everything I have learned over these years has come from many sources, including industry speakers and coaches, several of whom I will mention in this book. I will also recommend many phenomenal books that I have read, re-read, and continue to read. Just as significant is the wisdom I have gleaned from my mentors and friends in my Network Marketing business. I was also blessed to have a wonderful therapist, Leah D'voren, (may she Rest in Peace) who taught me the power of positive self-talk and affirmations, well before I became a Network Marketing Professional.

I don't believe in coincidences. I believe there's a force in the world that has a profound impact on who we are, what we do and more importantly, what we choose to think about. Some call it the Universe, some call it the "Law of Attraction" and others may call it God. It is certainly not an accident that I ended up in an industry that embraces personal development as a cornerstone to achieve maximum success. Who I am today, and what I have achieved these past 30+ years is directly correlated to my willingness to grow as a person and as a Network Marketing Professional.

30 years ago, I never would have imagined that I would write a book, and even more unimaginable, that the topic of the book would be creating success in the Network Marketing Industry. Over these past 3 decades, I have learned what to

do and more importantly, what not to do. I am confident that my experiences, some positive and some negative, can and will help you find success in your own Network Marketing business. So, as you read (or listen to) this book, I hope you will get value as I share the WEISER way to grow a Network Marketing business.

I had a powerful experience when I achieved a milestone, passing the 25-year mark in my Network Marketing company– yes, a quarter of a century with the same company. And how quickly those 25 years had passed! I can see in my mind's eye like it was yesterday, the day I was introduced to my company's products and income option. That day changed my life forever.

For a brief moment, I thought about retiring. Of course, those in the Network Marketing industry know we don't ever really retire in the traditional sense of the word, especially when we have built an organization that continues on and provides a substantial recurring revenue.

One of the great advantages of the Network Marketing business model is not only the money we earn now, but also money earned down the road for the work we do today. For example, if I do a brief product presentation to someone, who decides to become a consumer of my product and continues to purchase it each month or several times a year, my commission is earned on the products purchased each time they order. It's not necessary for me to do a product presentation to that same person each month to earn the commission. I only have to make that presentation one time. It's a similar scenario when an actor films a movie, commercial or TV show. They get paid each time that movie, TV show or commercial is broadcast which is like a royalty that continues to pay over time.

In November of 2017, I attended a Network Marketing conference, called GO PRO, with thousands of Network Marketing professionals. This is an annual event facilitated by industry leader, trainer and author, Eric Worre. Eric is an industry icon. He is a strategist and trainer to millions of top income earners in the Network Marketing industry. His book Go Pro, which outlines 7 steps to becoming a Network Marketing Professional is a must read for everyone who chooses to build a successful Network Marketing business. Go Pro is one of the first books I recommend to all my new business partners.

At that conference so many things were said that moved me, inspired me, and motivated me NOT to retire. On the contrary, I realized I had so much to share with people like you, who have chosen Network Marketing as their vehicle to have more time and earn additional income.

I was a camp director, nursery school music teacher, bar mitzvah tutor, actress and graduate student who said yes to a Network Marketing company. My hope is that after reading this book, you will have a better understanding of the nuances of Network Marketing and how it might serve you in reaching some of your goals. If you have been undecided whether or not the Network Marketing industry is a fit for you, I trust some of the tips I share in this book will support you in your decision to build and grow a successful business.

Donna J. Weiser

Chapter 1

EARLY LESSONS

Like many young Caucasian women born into an upper middle-class family in the 1950's, I was expected to get a college degree. But somewhere in the back of my mind, I briefly thought my path would be to marry a great guy, live in a house in "Suburbia USA" and stay at home to raise our children. That's what many women aspired to do in the 1950's. Early in the 1960's, women began entering the workforce in large numbers, and my mother was part of that movement. She worked part time as a bookkeeper, so I had a great role model of a woman who worked part time and raised her family. I knew I wanted to do something professionally and not "just" be a "housewife". However, my dilemma was that I didn't know what to do.

I loved music and singing and as a young girl I dreamed of being a Broadway Musical Star. Other than being in the chorus of a college production of *How to Succeed in Business Without Really Trying*, that dream never became a reality. I did, however, learn several important life lessons that would serve me well, many years later when I became a Network Marketing Professional.

My First Lesson was to Suit Up, Show Up, Do the Work, and Stay Out of the Results.

I have a nice voice, better than most. But just having a good voice wasn't enough to be in the chorus of a musical production, even a college production. You must be able to dance, and dancing was definitely not my forte. I had a terrible time learning the dance routine that I was expected to perform at the audition. However, I was determined to do well, so I asked another student who was a great dancer to teach me the dance routine. He broke down the dance moves step by step, and I spent much of the next 24 hours practicing, practicing and practicing. My desire to be on that stage was stronger than my fear of messing up at the audition. I showed up at that audition with a big smile on my face and did my very best. The next day, when they posted the cast list, guess whose name was listed as a member of the chorus? Yep. I was thrilled to see my name on that list. The director of the show pulled me aside and said, "I really appreciate how hard you tried. I saw that you struggled to learn the dance moves, but you improved overnight. If you are willing to work as hard as you did to learn those dance moves, I would love for you to be a member of our cast and join our production." He went on to say, "I loved your smile and your positive 'no matter what' attitude." It was quite rewarding for me to be acknowledged for the hard work and exceptional effort that I had put forth.

My second lesson from my musical production experience was to "be coachable".

When you first begin your Network Marketing business there is so much to learn–new language, new habits, and new skills. In our industry, you are in business for yourself, but not by yourself. Take advantage of those who came before. It's their job to support you in learning the new language, habits and skills.

By asking for support from those who have experienced success, you have a much better chance of experiencing your own success. I hadn't heard the expression, "be coachable" before I started my Network Marketing business; however, it was clear to me in all my endeavors over the years that reaching out to those who have more experience than me could only support me in my success.

"Being coachable" means you are leaving room for the possibility that there is something you haven't learned yet that could make you even better. It means that you're ready to do whatever it takes to change and improve in whatever situation you are in.

The beautiful thing about the industry of Network Marketing is that success truly comes to you when you help other people succeed. You are not bothering your upline sponsor or mentors when you ask questions. We love when new consultants or distributors ask questions. The more questions you ask, the more you will learn and the quicker you'll succeed.

For those who are new to this business, I recommend that you reach up to the person who recruited you, and if they are also new, reach up above them. There is someone, somewhere in your upline who has achieved significant success. Seek out that person and tell them that you are eager to learn, and you will do whatever they recommend. That's exactly what I did early on when I started my Network Marketing Business. I reached up, above 3 people, to find the person I wanted to be my mentor, to learn from and emulate. And to this day, not only is that person my mentor, but she has also become one of my dearest friends.

Once you find your mentor, then do what they recommend and be coachable. Do not make the mistake that many new recruits do by trying to "reinvent the wheel". Most established Network Marketing companies have a proven system that's already in place for you to follow.

And finally, as quickly as you can, become a student of the profession. Invest the time to study and learn. There are many excellent books about our industry that also support distributors. There are also many great speakers and trainers that you can find on YouTube as well as many excellent podcasts. Become competent, which leads to confidence. You will have so much more success when you are confident–confident about our industry, your company and yourself.

I was lucky, early on in my Network Marketing career to work with a fabulous author, speaker, mentor and coach who taught me an invaluable lesson that has supported me to this day. I was stuck and trying desperately to figure out why success was eluding me, then Sonia Stringer, a top flight business coach, taught me to focus more on my mindset and less on my activity. I was extremely busy doing so much activity, working non-stop and never taking a moment to breathe. More importantly, I never took time for personal development. Network Marketing is a business of attracting others to join us. From the outside looking in, I made it look way too hard. That was truly the beginning of my personal development journey in Network Marketing.

Takeaway Idea

Find Your Mentor & Be Coachable.

Take the Action

Reach out to the person who recruited you and if they are not actively building a business, reach out to someone above them. Explain that you are serious about achieving your goals and ask them if they would mentor you, help you be accountable and keep you on track.

Chapter 2

YOU ARE DOING *WHAT*??

I had limited exposure to Direct Sales or Network Marketing as a young woman. My mother briefly sold Avon when I was a little girl. I remember going with her each week, to deliver bags of "goodies" to the neighborhood ladies. My fondest memory of her brief Avon experience was playing with her makeup kit. I was eight years old. I recently asked my dad what motivated my mom to become an "Avon Lady" (That was the term they used back in the 1960's), and he said her motivation was simply to make some extra money. Making some "extra money" is a motivating factor for most people who start a Network Marketing business.

My mom was my number one supporter when I began my Network Marketing business. Perhaps her unconditional support had something to do with her Avon experience. I have no idea. But when everyone else thought I was crazy to drop out of graduate school and pursue my Network Marketing business, my mom cheered me on. I chose practical experience and immediate income potential rather than to delay.

My other exposure to direct sales or Network Marketing, other than attending a few Tupperware parties, was not a positive experience; and frankly, left me feeling quite distrustful about our industry. OK, here's the scene. I'm in San Francisco in Bloomingdale's department store, going down an escalator and I glance across at the people going up the other escalator. That's when I recognized one of my high school teachers. Our eyes met, we smiled, and she indicated that we should meet on the next floor. We embraced and started catching up. It was 1980, seven years after I graduated from high school.

Then, out of the blue, she asked me if I would like to come to a meeting to learn about "financial freedom"? I was taken back, surprised that she would ask me such an unusual question after chatting with me for less than five minutes. In the back of my mind I knew about Amway, so I asked, "Is this Amway"? And she looked at me and said, "not really". I pressed on, "well what is it? Is it like Amway"? She responded, "sort of". Now remember, I didn't have any experience with Network Marketing. I had never been approached or invited to attend an Amway meeting nor had I been to any other Network Marketing company's gathering. But I had heard about Amway. She told me if I attended this meeting I would learn about financial freedom and learn how I could own my own life. She encouraged me to come to the meeting, be her guest and just to trust her. I found it so interesting that she wanted me to trust her when she wasn't willing to be forthright about the meeting, or the company. I told her I was not willing to attend a meeting or a gathering without knowing what the meeting was all about. She then smiled sheepishly and said, well actually it is an Amway meeting. That was all I needed to hear, and I quickly responded with "No thank you, I have to get going. It was great to see you and best of luck."

After that encounter, I wanted nothing to do with an industry that wasn't forthcoming or honest about what they did or who they were. I'm certain that if she would have been forthright and honest about the company she represented from the very beginning of our conversation, there might have been a different outcome. There is a good chance that I would have attended that Amway meeting with her. The lesson is always to be upfront about our industry and the company we represent. My generation learned a great deal from Amway, one of the first Network Marketing companies, and today Amway is the #1 Network Marketing company in the world. That's something to be proud of!

Part of your job description as a Network Marketing professional is to be very proud of our industry and your company. Whenever you find yourself reading or listening to this book, you can easily grab the statistics from the DSA (Direct Selling Association) so you can share the real facts with your family, friends, and prospects. The statistics will solidify your belief, and subsequently, their belief that Network Marketing is a viable and very reputable industry.

When people ask if this is a pyramid, (and believe me, someone will) there are several responses you can give. Before I share a few suggested responses to this frequently asked question, understand that if you are defensive with your response, then the person you are talking to will become defensive too. You might handle this question by saying, Network Marketing is a legal business model, thanks in large part to Amway who long ago defended this business model in court. The industry is regulated by the Federal Trade Commission and other government agencies, but the two rules of thumb are these: Products must be presented and sold and the business is not built on sign-up fees alone. A good indicator of a reputable Network Marketing company is that sign-up fees are low as are inventory expenses or product purchases, if any.

One of the best responses I've heard to the question, "is this a pyramid", comes from industry expert Eric Worre. I have taken his lead and simply asked, Have you had an experience with Network Marketing? And then, keep your mouth shut and listen. Let them share, express their experiences and even vent, particularly if the experience was negative. Most people talk too much and don't listen. There's a reason you have two ears and one mouth. Listen twice as much as you speak and you will uncover so much by listening to their story and hearing their experience. You will uncover their objections, concerns, and perhaps even their fears. While talking to your prospect, be empathetic and understanding while sharing with them an important fact that probably never crossed their minds–that there are many, many Network Marketing companies, and even more Network Marketing distributors. Explain that all Network Marketing companies are not equal, just like any other business. If you have a bad experience with a doctor, does that mean you will never go to another doctor again? If you have a negative experience at a restaurant does that mean, you will never dine at another restaurant? Hopefully that will get them thinking. And then, you can ask permission to share why you believe your company or opportunity may be a great fit for them. Or, if not for them, then perhaps they can be an ambassador for you and introduce you to someone who might be a fit with your company.

Another excellent response to "Is this a pyramid" is to ask, "Tell me, what do you mean by a pyramid?" Once again, you are asking them a question, so listen carefully to their response. They may say, "Well, that's when the person at the top makes all the money." When someone gives me that response, I ask them where they work and what is the structure of their business. Who is the CEO, or the President of the company? How many people are part of upper management, and how many in middle management? How many people are entry level employees or lower management? Of course, many people don't work in a corporate structure, but I do the best I can to help them visualize a typical business or corporation. Then I ask, "what are the chances that someone in the sales division, or someone in lower or middle management could become the president or CEO of that company?" Most of the time the response is, "probably never". My response is, "I agree. Chances are slim that anyone in lower management could one day become the president of a large corporation." The structure of a corporation is a pyramid. The structure of a Network Marketing company is an inverted Pyramid. Each person who becomes a representative or distributor in a

Network Marketing company has an equal opportunity to rise to the top rank of their company.

There's room for many, many people to get to that top rank. It's never too late to jump in. That's not the case in the corporate model, where there's only room for one president or one CEO. There is also a level playing field in Network Marketing. People of all ages, genders, sexual preferences, races, religious affiliations, and nationalities are welcome and encouraged to build a Network Marketing business. A person with a high school diploma can rise to the top rank of their Network Marketing company as easily as someone with a doctorate or master's degree. No one asks to see your references or your resume. And depending on the time and effort a distributor puts into growing their business, they can rise to the top rank of the company rather quickly when and if they put in the hard work and effort.

Another response to the question "is this a pyramid", is to go right to what I said earlier. Simply smile and say, "of course not, pyramids are illegal. I would never invite you to be involved in anything illegal. Network Marketing is a multibillion-dollar global industry. Definitely not illegal. If you would allow me, I would be happy to share some facts and information about this exciting industry that I'm so proud to be a part of."

Takeaway Idea
Know Your Business, and always be ready to explain the Network Marketing model.

Take the Action
Review the books (at the back of this book) on Network Marketing to better understand the business model. Learn the benefits and features of Network Marketing and study what sets your company apart from the competition so you are confident when someone questions your decision and asks if you are part of a pyramid.

Chapter 3

THE LIST

PEOPLE ARE LOOKING FOR SOMETHING,

YOU'RE LOOKING FOR SOMEONE

Most people begin their Network Marketing business making a list of 50 to 100 people they know. This list is made up of the people they will initially contact to share their business and product. When I began my business, I was given the acronym FRANK, as a memory jogger to help me complete my list.

F - Friends
R - Relatives
A - Acquaintances
N - Neighbors
K - Kids

As I mentioned earlier, I was quite concerned with what people would think of my decision to build a Network Marketing business; therefore, I was reluctant to ask friends and family to look at my products and income option. If I wasn't willing to speak to family and friends (also known as our warm market, the people we know) then I had to learn the skill to talk to people I didn't know (also known as our cold market; people we don't know).

I was determined to create a successful business with or without the help of my warm market. I would not allow their possible negativity to dissuade me from taking my business to the top. My intention was to find people to buy my products and join my team.

I made a commitment to find leads. I even joined several formal networking groups. But I found that I was having more success meeting people and finding prospects when I was "out and about", because I learned an important skill: "how to warm up the cold market" by talking with perfectly good strangers.

My first tip to help you "warm up the cold market" is, get clear on your intention. Before you walk out the door, your intention must be crystal clear. The intention that you are looking for people must be at the forefront of your mind. You are looking for people to share the best product or service on the market, and you're looking for people to share the best opportunity in the industry.

Most people have no idea that they're looking for something. They only know that they're dissatisfied with something in their lives. For many people, it's debt. For others who are lucky enough to have a good paying job, they don't have enough time to spend with those they love. Some of the people you will meet, out and about, have been praying for something in their lives; they are just not sure what. The law of attraction is simple yet powerful. If they're looking for something and you're looking for someone, there's a strong chance that you're going to meet. Start off with that clear intention, the intention that you are going to find someone who would benefit from your product, service or income option. If your intention isn't clear, they just might walk right past you.

When it comes to social media, you must have the same intention. The intention is that you will meet someone on social media who is looking for something, and that "something" might just be your product, service or opportunity!

How do you make your intention clear? Since our minds are so powerful, that's where you start. You must affirm what you want to create, including getting names of people (we'll call them "leads") to share your product or business. By creating an affirmation that supports exactly what you want to create, you have a much better chance of connecting with the right people. "I am guided to connect with the right people at the right time." That's an example of one of my daily affirmations. I recite several affirmations each morning to focus my mind and activity. If you are looking for affirmations, you can search the internet. This is just one example. When I begin my day with that affirmation, I have created the intention to connect with the "right" people throughout the day. It makes a huge difference when you leave your home with a clear intention. And for those who are using social media as a prospecting tool, this affirmation is equally effective for you. You will be guided to connect with the right people, at the right time on whatever social media platform you are using.

The second tip is, do not prejudge. Please don't say no for someone before they do. They just might say "yes" . It's human nature to assume a negative response when you ask them to take a look at your product, service or opportunity. However, you have no idea what's going on in their lives and it might be the perfect time for them to hear about what you have to offer.

The third tip is to authentically give someone a compliment. This will help you build rapport. And rapport is the name of the game, when you are out and about, meeting people you don't know. Find something genuine about them to compliment. If you are at a retail store, restaurant or anywhere someone is giving you excellent service, then compliment them sincerely. "Thanks for giving me such great service". Or "You have a great personality, and it looks like you really love what you do." Ask lots of questions, ie: How long have you worked here? What did you do before you worked here? What do you like about working here? If they are someone who looks like they take great care of themselves, give them a compliment, and say, "you look fantastic. You look like someone who takes great care of yourself."

At this point, listen to their response. It's important when you are "warming up the cold market" to really listen and you will have a better understanding of what their needs are. Once you make your statement, keep quiet and listen to their response.

The fourth tip is to bring three words into the conversation which will allow you to mention your Network Marketing business in a favorable way. The three powerful words are "in my business." When you use the words "in my business," people are inclined to ask you, "what's your business?" Does it happen every time? Of course not. However, in my experience, 90% of the time, using the words "in my business" will prompt someone to ask what you do. Now they've opened the door for you to tell them what you do. You want to practice your response, so you feel comfortable and confident, yet at the same time, you want to be authentic and not seem rehearsed. Share with them that you are a Network Marketing professional and that you represent company XYZ. Then ask if they have heard of the company. Notice I am being 100% open, honest and forthright. Be proud that you are a Network Marketing professional.

Examples of how "in my business" follows the above example. "You give such great customer service; I notice that in my business." "You have such a great personality; I notice that in my business."

Once again, you can use the same formula while dialoguing with people on social media. But, since you are not face to face and you can have an opportunity to "chat" with them again, you can build rapport over several days. On social media, sometimes it will be weeks before you feel authentically compelled to bring up your business. I heard a great analogy to building rapport and not bringing up your business immediately. You don't ask someone to marry you on the first date, so why bring up your business in the first communication. Be sure to keep track of who you have been communicating with, follow their posts, genuinely comment on their posts and when it's appropriate, give them the compliment and proceed. If you bring it up too quickly, you'll just be a "Network Marketing scammer" and those people give our industry a bad name.

As I previously mentioned, I did not feel supported by family and friends when I began my business. I was intent on getting leads, so I went out every day, and met "strangers" at the mall, at the park, at coffee shops, and at the gym. These people weren't strangers by the time we finished speaking. I reached the second highest rank in my business "warming up the cold market".

Initially ask your sponsor to support you in talking to your friends and acquaintances about your new business and products. This can be done in person or virtually. They know more and have practiced more times than you. Ask a contact who knows you, if you could "practice" with them. Listen to your sponsor and learn while you earn. Ask your sponsor to do a presentation with you to see how it is done. Remember your sponsor may make it look easy to reach out and talk to people, but they have just faced down fear and learned to manage it in order to reach their goals.

Takeaway Idea
This is a relationship business. Meet people everywhere.

Take the Action
You probably have many more contacts in your phone or social media than you think. Make a list of 100 people who may be interested in your product, service or income option. Do not prejudge. Don't say NO for someone before they say NO to you. Ask your upline to help you with the proper verbiage to reach out. Even if someone is on your chicken list, meaning someone you are afraid to reach out to, reach out anyway. Tell them you admire and respect them and would be so happy to get their feedback or opinion.

Chapter 4

DON'T TAKE THE NO'S PERSONALLY

In Network Marketing you will probably find yourself in situations that may be initially disappointing. You must be resilient and not take these disappointments to heart. You may ask someone to "take a look" at your opportunity, your product or service, and they promise to get back to you and never do. Or you may set up an appointment to get together with someone who agreed to meet with you (either in person or virtually); and not only did they not show up, they also didn't have the courtesy to let you know they weren't showing up. You may develop a great rapport with someone on social media and suddenly, they ghost you. Even more frustrating is when you enroll a new member to join your team and they are so excited to get started but end up MIA after a few days. If you are willing to accept these disappointments and not take them personally (I repeat, NOT take them personally) and continue to reach out to people and schedule appointments over and over and over again, I can almost guarantee that one of the appointments WILL hold. And perhaps that person may just become your next ACE!

ACE - In a deck of cards, there are four aces, picture cards, number cards and 2 jokers. If I asked you to shuffle the cards and then turn them over, one at a time, until you found an ACE, some might find an ace immediately, after turning over one, two or three cards. Others may have to turn over 10, 11 or maybe even 12 or 13 cards before they find their ACE. One thing we know for sure is that there are definitely 4 ACEs in that deck of cards. If you give up too soon, you'll never turn over an ACE.

So, what's the definition of an ACE in Network Marketing? Someone who is determined to take this business all the way to the top. They have vision and are self-starters. They have integrity. They are true to their word. They go the extra mile. Perhaps they already have a great network (or they are willing to build one). They have a willingness to work hard, they are coachable, and they have a 'no matter what' attitude.

By the way, do these qualities describe you? If not, you have a great place to start. Work on becoming an ACE yourself.

Another lesson is to keep setting up appointments and if someone doesn't show up, say a silent little prayer, wishing them well. Reach out with a message so they know you care and are checking in. Give them another opportunity to get together with you, either in person or virtually.

Your business is your priority, NOT your prospects (or anyone else's).

In my first year in my Network Marketing business, I had an appointment to share my products and business opportunity with a grocery checker whom I'd met at a local supermarket. We were scheduled to meet at my home, on a Wednesday evening and when she didn't show up to our confirmed appointment, I was annoyed; really annoyed. My husband had taken our kids out for the evening so I could have the house to myself. Remember, I was new at this business and thought I had to do everything perfectly.

I called this young woman several times and left messages over the next few days. She never returned my calls. That weekend, I found myself back in the supermarket for my weekly grocery shopping. I didn't see the checker who "stood me up", so I asked the manager if she was scheduled to work that day. He looked shocked and quite dismayed at my question and responded with, “I’m so sorry to have to tell you this, but she was killed in a car accident on Tuesday night.” What??? I was completely taken back. That was the day before she was supposed to meet with me. The day her family and friends were mourning her loss, I was annoyed at her for not showing up at my house. That was a huge lesson for me. If someone stands me up or doesn’t show, I always say a silent prayer that all is well.

In this day of texting, messaging and using smart phones, tablets, and computers to communicate with our prospects, it’s so important to realize how easy it is for someone NOT to receive your message. I recommend, if you don’t hear back from someone within 48 hours, reach back to them again. I can’t tell you how many times I have missed texts or messages because I didn’t hear the alert, or a more important or pressing message came in afterwards. How many times have you seen a message on your phone, glanced at it quickly, and gave yourself a silent reminder to respond back when you have time? How many times have you forgotten to go back to a message and several days later you see it and you’re horrified because you never responded? That happens to me so often and I’m sure it happens to you as well. I find it interesting that most people go right toward the worst-case scenario, thinking that someone is standing them up or ghosting them. My advice is to think more rationally and assume the best, not the worst.

The reality is that our business is a numbers game. I love the mantra, some will, some won’t, so what, Next? I’ve heard a few different statistics about how many prospects we have to reach out to in order to find a new distributor. Here’s an average: Reach out to 10, perhaps 5 or 6 will get back to you. Of those 5 or 6, perhaps 3 or 4 will agree to meet with you (in person or virtually) and of those 3 or 4 with whom you meet, perhaps 1 might become a product user or business partner. I know those aren’t great odds, but it’s the truth. And, it’s also the reason that we must keep adding more names to our list. And, why it's important to embrace the NO's, because behind every NO is a YES.

If I was writing this book 30 years ago, we wouldn't be discussing people "ghosting" us or not answering our text messages. When I began my Network Marketing business in 1992, only the elite and very wealthy had cell phones, so texting wasn't an option. Motorola was the first company to produce a handheld mobile phone. On April 3, 1973, Martin Cooper, a Motorola researcher and executive, made the first mobile telephone call from handheld subscriber equipment, placing a call to Dr. Joel S. Engel of Bell Labs, his rival.

Then in 1984, Somewhere in either Chicago, Baltimore or Washington, someone plunked down $3,995 to buy the Motorola DynaTAC 8000X, the first handheld cell phone. (Imagine spending $4000 to purchase a cell phone today?) It wasn't until 1996, when mobile phones became more accessible to the public.

For that matter, can you even conceive of building a Network Marketing business or any business today without cell phones? When I started my Network Marketing business, we only used land lines and fax machines.

Takeaway Idea
It's a Numbers Game.

Take the Action
Grab a clean 16 oz jar from your kitchen. Label it *"NO's TO SUCCESS"*. Everytime someone says NO to you, put a penny in that jar. There's a very good chance that by the time that jar is filled with pennies, you will have advanced at least one rank in your business.

Chapter 5

SURVIVING SELF DOUBT

In High School I discovered one of my gifts was leadership.

My favorite definition of leadership is the ability to influence others. Thank you, John Maxwell, for that wonderful definition.

I was never a great student, and I didn't love academia in high school. Sports wasn't my thing either, so I quickly got involved in student government and eventually became the student body president of Taft High, a large public high school in Woodland Hills (a suburb of Los Angeles, California).

In 1973 at my high school graduation, I addressed the student body and their parents, an audience of over 5,000 people. As the student body president, I spoke of the hopes and dreams of those in the class and how "we" (the collective we) would change the world. Listening to me address my peers, their friends, and families on that beautiful June afternoon, no one would have ever believed that I suffered with low self-esteem and a deep sense of unworthiness. Looking from the outside in, most people would have thought the opposite. Why? Because I was popular, positive, and outgoing. So how does one become the Student Body President of one of the largest high schools in Southern California, and yet feel deeply unworthy with a very low self-image? Often, what you see on the outside doesn't reflect what's happening on the inside. I went to sleep many, many nights filled with self-doubt and sadness. Needless to say, self-esteem and self-worth are complicated issues.

Self-esteem is simply how you feel about yourself and how you judge your worth. This evaluation has a profound impact on the choices you make since it determines to a great extent what you consider yourself capable and worthy of doing.

I left high school and went directly to the University of Santa Barbara in Southern California. For many, that might have been a great move, but for me it was the beginning of a very tough and challenging next several years. I went from being a big fish in a little sea to a little fish in a big ocean, and my ego couldn't handle that. Over the next few years, I dropped out of college, (My parents weren't happy with that decision) got a job working as a receptionist for a prominent CPA firm in Beverly Hills and pursued a singing career.

A year and a half later, I felt compelled to go back to college and probably broke the world's record for the number of colleges and universities one person could attend during their entire college career. Eventually, I earned a Bachelor of Science degree in recreation administration from Cal State University at Long Beach. Even with that degree, my dilemma remained the same. The question that I continued to struggle with was, "what should I do with my life that would have purpose and meaning?"

What does this discussion about self-worth and self-esteem have to do with your Network Marketing business? Everything! Having a strong sense of self-worth and a high self-esteem are important qualities to possess if you want to become a successful Network Marketing Professional. In my experience, you must embrace personal development to reach the highest rank or level in your company. This is not an option. This is non-negotiable.

When you have a Network Marketing business, you are your own boss. If YOU are the boss, when you wake up in the morning and you look in the mirror, you are looking at the boss. If you don't like the boss, then you are in trouble. The good news is, if you are reading this book and you doubt yourself, have low self-esteem, or not much self-worth, there is absolute hope for a positive transformation. Many Network Marketing companies pride themselves in being a "personal development company" that just happens to sell a phenomenal product or service.

You can change your self-talk and the way you look and feel about yourself. It's 100% up to you and your choice. You can roll up your sleeves and get to work on becoming the best version of yourself. By the way, becoming the best version of yourself and becoming a successful Network Marketing Professional DOES take work. "Success only comes before work in the dictionary."

> According to Marketdata, LLC, The U.S. self-improvement market was worth $11.6 billion in 2019, vs $9.38 billion in 2016. It is forecast to grow 6.0% per year, on average between 2019 and 2025, when the market should be worth $14.0 billion. That's quite an uptrend.

I spent many years in and out of therapy, personal development seminars and 12-step meeting rooms. How I ended up with low self-esteem and how that manifested in my life is a topic for another book. For the purpose of this book, I will sum it up briefly.

I carried around baggage for many years due to old messages that I perceived as truth. My self-talk was filled with feelings of lack and doubt. A big factor in my recovery from a deep sense of unworthiness came from several therapy sessions around Transactional Analysis (or TA as it is often called). It's a model of people and relationships that was developed during the 1960's by Dr. Eric Berne. Over the years, with the support of therapists, life coaches and much introspective work, I came to realize those negative messages did not serve me. I hope this is great news for many of you who continue to hold on to negative thoughts. One of the reasons that I love our industry is that most successful Network Marketing professionals not only embrace personal development, but they also become students of personal growth. I can't encourage you enough to pick up a personal development book immediately and start reading. Many, many people have overcome worthiness issues, feelings of self-doubt, and fear by reading and studying several of the books recommended in the appendix. As a matter of fact, the first book I read when I joined my Network Marketing business was *Feel the Fear and Do it Anyway*, by Dr. Susan Jeffers. I was petrified to pick up the phone and call a lead or a prospect. However, I understood that if I didn't reach out to my prospects or leads, I would never create a successful business. For those who continue to suffer from the pangs of self-doubt and low self-esteem, I would suggest reaching out to a therapist or professional counselor to help you uncover how to overcome your feelings of unworthiness and negative self-talk.

There are a number of notables, premier among them is Shad Helmstetter, author of *What to Say When You Talk to Yourself*. They know that our inner conversation and "self talk" influences us everyday and is often determinative. Shad teaches us that we can often combat negative self talk by writing some positive affirmations to alleviate the doubt that we may be experiencing.

IMPORTANT - The affirmation must be written in the present tense. When you state "I WILL be a successful network marketer, you are giving yourself permission to wait. Instead, state it in the present tense: **I AM a successful Network Marketer.**

Here are a few more examples:

OLD MESSAGE - No one wants to join my team.

NEW AFFIRMATION - People are excited to partner with me.

OLD MESSAGE: People never call me back.

NEW AFFIRMATION: People are excited to hear from me and always call me back.

Takeaway Idea
Embrace Personal Development and Choose Belief over Doubt.

Take the Action
Make a list of any self doubting thoughts regarding your business. Next, create affirmations that are the opposite of the self doubting thoughts. Write the affirmations in the present tense. Write the new affirmations twice a day for 30 days. Read them with emotion and feeling.

Chapter 6

YOU'RE THE BRAND

HOW TO MARKET YOURSELF

In 1992, my daughters were 6 and 9 years old. We were living in Southern California and my kids were attending an excellent elementary school. Junior High School was a few short years away and I desperately wanted them to attend a local private school. I have no idea what private school tuition is where you live, but in Southern California private tuition is like having another mortgage (and mortgages in Southern California are already exorbitant). I was a camp director, earning about $35,000 a year and supplemented my income by tutoring children for their Bar and Bat Mitzvahs. Thinking an MBA would be the answer to my financial woes, I enrolled in graduate school for a Master's in Business. I was fortunate that I didn't have to take a loan for graduate school, but I am in the minority.

> According to studentloanhero.com, as of January 2021, Americans are more burdened by student loan debt than ever. Among the class of 2019, 69% of college students took out student loans, and they graduated with an average debt of $29,900 including both private and federal debt. Meanwhile, 14% of their parents took out an average of $37,200 in federal parent PLUS loans. And finally, here's a scary statistic: Americans owe over $1.71 trillion in student loan debt, spread out among about 44.7 million borrowers. That's about $739 billion more than the total United States credit card debt.

Today more than ever, people understand the importance of diversification. This is a technique that reduces risk by allocating investments among various financial instruments, industries and other categories. Think of starting a Network Marketing business as another way to add to your portfolio.

In 1999, the IRS reinstated the favorable tax treatment of home office deductions, and helped make tax planning more attractive for networkers. According to Jeff Babener, Babener & Associates/MLMLegal.com, if you take your Network Marketing business seriously, you may qualify for some serious tax advantages that are available to business owners, and in particular, home-based business owners. With that in mind and knowing tax regulations change, be sure to talk to an accountant or CPA to find out what benefits you can enjoy as a Network Marketing Professional.

I always remind the people whom I invite to join my business that this is a "snickers decision" not a "mortgage decision". I also encourage them to treat their new endeavor in Network Marketing as a business and not a hobby. Hobbies cost money and businesses (when they are treated as such) have the potential to earn money.

The same year that I enrolled in graduate school, I also decided to pursue an acting career. I performed in a musical production at an Overeaters Anonymous Convention in the early 1990's. The show was called THIN LINES, which was a clever parody of "A Chorus Line". A well-known actor, who was also in the show, told me he thought I was talented and encouraged me to pursue an acting career. I had a good "mom look", so I figured if I booked a few commercials, it would alleviate some of the financial stress we were experiencing. In 1992, in addition to going to graduate school, I enrolled in several acting classes to support my new "acting career". Having a Type-A personality, if I was going to study acting, I was committed to giving it 100%, with the end goal to book a commercial or a role on a TV show.

Speaking of Type A personalities, here are some characteristics of a Type A personality: A temperament characterized by excessive ambition, more competitive, highly organized, impatient, and highly aware of time management. Can you relate to those attributes? When I write affirmations and visualize the type of person I want to enroll into my Network Marketing business, these qualities are at the top of my list.

One of the classes I took during my brief pursuit as an actor was how to market yourself to casting directors, producers, and directors. The theory behind the following exercise is to help you discover your "true essence". Essence is the intrinsic nature or indispensable quality of something, especially something abstract, that determines its character.

The purpose of the exercise was to learn how the world sees us and our qualities. It was a fascinating exercise and I highly recommend you do this to support your Network Marketing business. It's important to know how you are viewed by others and the world around you.

For this exercise, all you need is a partner, a clip board, a list of character traits and a couple of hours. (You can search the internet for a list of character traits for this exercise.)

Put that list on a clipboard, grab your partner and head out to a few locations where there's a crowd of people whom you don't know. (Example of locations for this exercise: Hotel lobby, college campus, busy park, or shopping mall.) Person A is standing 10 - 20 feet away. Person B, who has the clipboard, approaches a stranger and says, "Hi, I'm taking a marketing class and wonder if you can help me. Do you see that person standing over there in jeans and blue top? That's my friend Steve. I have a quick survey for you. Take a look at Steve, and then quickly go over this list of character traits and without any conversation and not knowing my friend, check off all the words that come to mind when you look at Steve."

After doing this exercise, (and a few more in-depth exercises), these were my character traits. "Takes the bull by the horn," "confident," "nutty," "pretty as a picture," and "happy as a clam."

Find 50 people to take this survey and you may be surprised how the world sees you!

Takeaway Idea
Learn how to Brand and Market Yourself.

Take the Action
Search the internet for a list of Character Traits and print out the list. Grab a partner and do the exercise mentioned above in this chapter.

Chapter 7

MEETING NEW PEOPLE

ALWAYS CHOOSE COURAGE

I had an acquaintance who was an assistant director on a well-known ABC Soap Opera, General Hospital. She couldn't get me a speaking part but told me that I could be an extra on the show. (An extra on a TV show or movie is a person in the background; a person who has no speaking lines, but their presence is needed for the scene) I suited up and showed up at the set of General Hospital and spent 2 days sitting in a "pretend" restaurant, having "pretend" conversations with other extras on my favorite Soap Opera. (It was so exciting for me, since I had been a fan of General Hospital since moving to California in 1968.) My intention was to have a speaking part on TV, so I asked one of the other "extra's", "How does someone who is an extra get a speaking role on this soap opera?" He looked at me like I had two heads. "You don't" he responded quite adamantly. He continued, "extras do not, under any circumstances, get a speaking role on TV shows. We are not actors, we are extras."

Well, maybe that was HIS truth, but my intention was clear. And being my persistent, Type A personality self, I was up for the challenge of proving this man wrong.

At this point in my acting career, I hadn't done much acting. But I did have a VHS recording of myself doing a monologue from an acting class. There was a short break one of the days that I was on set as an extra, so I made my way up to the casting office. I popped my head in the door and as luck would have it, the casting director was just walking out of the casting office when I arrived. I don't believe in luck or coincidences, but I do believe in the "Law of Attraction" and my intention was crystal clear that afternoon. As Wayne Dyer, one of my favorite authors, states, "my intentions create my reality". I smiled and said, "Hi, I'm Donna Weiser and I'm on set today as an extra. I wanted to share a video of a monologue that I did in my acting class, with hopes that you might find a role for me on the show?" She smiled back and said, "Thanks, I'll take a look and let you know. " It was now time for me to be bold and ask her if I could get back to her. I said, "may I call you and see what you thought of the video?" Most people would not have had the courage to ask that question. Most people would have said "great, I'll look forward to hearing from you". But my intention was too strong to let fear get the best of me. I was thrilled when she responded positively and said, "Sure, here's my number. Give me a call in a couple of days."

This concept of asking for what you want, being bold, and then staying out of the results is really an important concept to support you in growing your Network Marketing business. Remember if you don't ask, the answer is always "No". I love Hockey Hall of Famer, Wayne Gretzky's famous quote, "you miss 100% of the shots you don't take!"

I was committed to getting a speaking part on that soap opera, so I was bold when I asked the casting director if I could call her. Two days later I picked up the phone, dialed her number and said, "Hi Linda, this is Donna Weiser calling. If you recall, I gave you the video of my monologue from my acting class on Monday. I was wondering if you had a chance to watch it?"

You can use a similar approach when you're calling a prospect or a lead. "Hi Bob, this is Donna Weiser calling. If you recall, we met at the park on Tuesday when our kids were playing. I was just calling to see if you had a chance to watch that video I sent you?" Same principle. Be bold, ask the question and then stay out of the results.

So, back to the casting director. Her response, when I asked if she had watched my video , was "no, not yet", I've been so busy.

Now, I had a choice, once again. Courage or fear?

I chose courage over fear and faith over doubt. I took a deep breath and asked if I could call her in the next few days and she said, "sure". So, that's exactly what I did. I called her back in 3 days and asked if she had a chance to watch the video and her response was "it's been crazy around here". Once again, I put on my "courage hat" and asked if I may call her back in the next few days and once again, she said "sure".

Would you have continued to ask if you were me? Ryan Blair, author and entrepreneur, said, "If it's important you'll find a way; if not, you will find an excuse." I love that quote. As a matter of fact, it's taped on my desktop computer to remind me every day NOT to buy into excuses. Getting a speaking role on that TV show was extremely important to me, so once again, I picked up the phone and called because, believe it or not, tenacity builds trust. The third time I called, her assistant answered the phone and told me Linda was out with the flu. I waited a week and called her again. The first thing I asked when she picked up the phone, was how was she feeling? And she told me how sick she had been, that her whole family had been ill. We spent a few minutes chatting, building rapport and discussing our families.

Here's another important tip when it comes to prospecting and calling your leads. Be genuinely interested in what's going on in your prospect's life. Ask lots of questions. Remember to be more interested than interesting.

After Linda and I chatted about our families, when it felt appropriate and I sensed the right moment, I asked if she had a chance to watch the video from my acting class. She apologized and said that she had not. She had been so behind since she missed a week of work due to her illness. I wished her a good week and told her I would reach out next week and she said, “perfect, let’s connect next week.” I made a note on my calendar to call her the following week, which is exactly what I did! The next week, I did what I said I would do. I called and asked if she had had a chance to watch the video and her response was much more hopeful. She promised she would watch the video that day and would I please call back the following day. I called back the following day, with a smile in my voice and hope in my heart and said, “Hi Linda, it’s Donna Weiser calling. I’m just following up to see if you had a chance to watch the video.”

Meeting and prospecting new people, people I didn’t know became a speciality of mine. Prospecting your “cold market” is a valuable skill and it is where great growth is possible. I use a very similar approach and language when following up with someone new who has samples of my product, information about the company’s service and/or income option. Here’s how I follow up with a prospect and I never let myself anticipate their response, be it positive or negative: “Hi Sally, this is Donna Weiser calling. If you recall, we met on Thursday at Starbucks. I sent you some information about my company’s income option, and I’m wondering if you had an opportunity to take a look”?

Here is a critical piece of advice after I ask the question: I am patient and let them answer. It can feel very awkward, but I wait for their response.

Our business is a numbers game and you’re setting yourself up for failure if you take the time to share your products, business or service but don’t follow up. Continue to follow up, building trust until someone tells you to stop. The fortune truly is in the follow up. I even go so far as to say to someone who has not returned a call or text, “ “Hey, I’ve left you several messages and since I haven't heard back I'm sure it's one of 3 things, 1 - you are so very busy and you haven't had a moment to get back to me, and I get it, I'm super busy too. 2 - you aren't interested in my products, business, service (you fill in the correct word for your situation) or 3 - and I hope it's not 3 - I hope I didn't say or do anything to offend you. People usually respond very quickly when I leave that message and apologize for not getting back to me. Thanks to author and speaker Michael Durkin for this excellent tool to use when people don't return your calls or texts.

My experience shows me 9 times out of 10, your prospects or leads will not tell you to stop reaching out. According to Brevet, a sales consulting firm, 80% of sales require five follow-up calls after the first meeting. 44% of sales reps give up after 1 follow-up. I can't begin to tell you how many people thanked me profusely for my pleasant persistence in following up. My advice is just to keep going for as IRC Sales Solutions reports:

- 92% of salespeople give up after no sales on the 4th call
- 60% of customers say no four times before saying yes

So back to Linda, the casting director. When I called the following day, she laughed and said, "Donna, I really appreciate your persistence. I am going to watch it right now. Please call me back in an hour".

I called an hour later, and she told me that she liked the video and that I had a great look. I thanked her and asked what was the next step? She said she would reach out to me when something came up.

I was thrilled and at the same time, a bit nervous because I had no reason to call her again. We had built such a great rapport over the course of several weeks and now the ball was completely in her court.

A similar phenomenon happens in our Network Marketing business after we conclude a business presentation. When our prospect expresses some interest and closes the conversation with, "I'll get back to you" we are often at a loss of what to say next. One of the tools that I use to avoid that uncomfortable moment when we aren't quite sure what to say next is to use a scale from 1 to 10. This scale is to gauge not only the prospect's interest level, but their desire to join your business. I often will say, "Steve, on a scale from 1 to 10, 10 - you can't wait to join me in becoming my business partner, and 1 - you never want to see me or hear of my company ever again (I laugh when I say this). Where are you?"

Now comes the hard part. It's been said, "when you are working a deal, the first one to speak loses." So, bite your tongue or do whatever you have to do, NOT to speak and let them give you their number, from 1- 10. They may take several seconds to answer and those several seconds may feel like several minutes.

After they give you their number, you have a better understanding of their interest level. You can then ask, "is there any other information I can provide, to help you move from a 7 to a 10 (or from a 6 to a 9). And once again, put on your listening cap and let them speak.

Thanks to marketing and sales consultant, Ike Krieger, for teaching me this tool in the early years of building my business. It has never steered me wrong.

Here is another excellent tool that I learned from one of my mentors, mindset coach and Network Marketing Industry expert, Jerry Roisentul. Once again, after your formal presentation has ended, you can say with a big smile on your face, "Sue, before I let you go, based on what you've seen (or heard) today, does this look like something you could see yourself doing, IF you had the proper coaching, training, and support?

Now keep going and don't pause to wait for an answer. Continue with, "in my experience, most people fall into one of three categories after I do this presentation. Category #1 is, "yes, tell me what the next step is to get started." Category #2 is, "It sounds great, but I still have some questions" and the 3rd Category is, "It does make sense, but it's not for me, or the timing isn't good for me right now." So, Steve, based on what you have heard today, which category best describes you?

If they say, #1, then YAY, you have a new business partner. If they say #2, then you are tasked to answer their questions so they can make an informed decision. If their response is #3, get them on your product or service immediately as a customer. And ask for permission to check back with them, sometime in the near future, to revisit looking at your income option.

Whatever category they fall into, be sure to end with, "Now you can see why I am so excited about my company and my business."

When the casting director, Linda, told me she would reach out to me, I was filled with doubt and fear. But what could I do? Just like in our business, we must have faith and trust the process. Our job is to plant the seeds and then, we stay out of the results.

A few weeks later, I was at an audition for a TV commercial when my pager beeped. (Back in the early 90's we had pagers, not cell phones). I headed to the nearest payphone, grabbed a quarter, and dialed the number that appeared on the tiny screen. By the way, I did not recognize the number that flashed on my pager.

After a few rings, someone picked up and said, “General Hospital casting”. I was beside myself with excitement, the same excitement that I get in my Network Marketing business when I get an email, call, or text, from a prospect who tells me they are ready to get started!

The great news is, I did have the opportunity to appear on General Hospital several times. Setting a goal and achieving it was an invaluable lesson for me. You can also learn to suit up and show up, but remember to stay out of the results!

Takeaway Idea

Your Cold Market is Rich with Possibilities and People. If you resist reaching out to perfectly good strangers, many opportunities will be missed. Cold Market prospecting is a skill and you can grow to enjoy it. Remember your job is to care, build rapport, make new acquaintances and add names to your list.

Take the Action

Carve out time each week to explore the “cold market”. Use some of the skills discussed in this chapter and make it fun to meet new people. Don’t worry if they say NO, because there is always a YES coming.

Chapter 8

COMMIT TO A GOAL

"A goal without a deadline is just another dream." These are brilliant words by Canadian businessman, investor and television personality, Robert Herjavec. There are many books and articles written about Goals. I recommend that you carve out time to think about, write down and visualize achieving your goals.

Where do you want to be in five years? Where do you want to be in one year? 6 months, 3 months, 1 month, 1 week? It's important to have a big goal for the future which is part of your vision and it's equally important to do something tomorrow that will help you move toward that goal.

Tony Robbins says, "Setting GOALS is the first step in turning the invisible into the VISIBLE."

Here is a great visual. You have made the decision to drive across the United States. Your goal is to get to New York, and your starting point is across the country in Los Angeles. Your first step is to decide how you are going to get from Los Angeles to New York. You have several options. You can fly, you can drive, or you can even walk (if you have the time to do so). For our example, let's say you have decided to drive. But even that decision leaves you with several options. Are you going to drive directly through the center of the country? Or take a northern route, or perhaps a southern route? Are you going to drive by yourself or are you going to invite someone to join you? Each decision you make includes a choice and an action plan.

Can you imagine just hopping in the car without any plan? Would you go to the airport without a reservation? What about leaving on a trip where you'll be gone for several days without packing a suitcase? These options all require a thoughtful plan of action. But before any of these things can happen, you first must decide. Your first decision was deciding that you wanted to travel across the country.

Every goal you set for yourself starts with a decision, and behind that decision is your reason WHY. One of my favorite books is *Start With Why* by Simon Sinek. Your WHY is your central belief. It's the concept that motivates you to get out of bed in the morning. It's what moves you to take action. When your WHY is clear, the HOW presents itself. Get clear on your WHY and it will be much easier to set your goals.

Is there a magic formula to goal setting? As it turns out, there is. A study from the Dominican University of California concentrated not only on goal setting, but on the actual strategies for achieving goals. Best of all, this study concluded with measurable results. The group that followed this specific model reaped the best results:

1. **Commit to Action.** Rather than simply writing down a goal, the group was asked to commit to an action. This included filling out a survey leading them through a thorough thought process to develop goals and setting concrete action commitments. Essentially, they were making a commitment, on paper, to achieve their goal.

2. **Accountability to Peers.** The group was tasked to follow up their concrete goal planning and action commitment by enlisting another person to support them. They needed to send their commitment to a peer, making them more accountable.

3. **Regular Updates.** The group members updated their friend or accountability partner on a weekly basis, which kept them focused on their progress.

Dr. Gail Matthews, who ran the Dominican University of California study, stated:

> My study provides empirical evidence for the effectiveness of three coaching tools: accountability, commitment, and writing down one's goals.

I used this formula when I began my Network Marketing Business and continue to use it today. I feel accomplished when I write down my goals, commit to an action plan and declare my goal to an accountability partner. I'm convinced that this formula has been a contributing factor to the success I have created in my business.

Takeaway Idea
Goals = Growth.

Take the Action
Reach out to your upline to help define which goals will support you in creating success in your business immediately. Use Good, Great and Awesome Goals as your guide. Your Good Goal is your bottom line commitment. This is a goal you will achieve "no matter what", so be sure it's a goal that is reachable and achievable. Your Great Goal is a bit of a stretch, a goal that will push you out of your comfort zone. And your Awesome Goal is the dream. The sky's the limit so dream big.

Chapter 9

PERSONAL GROWTH

A NEW EDUCATION

As I mentioned earlier in this book, I attended several colleges and universities over the course of my college career. I even dropped out of college for a short time to pursue a singing career, because I didn't believe I had the skills to be a successful college student.

When I was 10, my dad's company transferred him to Chicago and my family moved from Cherry Hill, New Jersey to Glenview, Illinois. In N.J., I was just learning how to do multiplication in my 3rd grade class, but when I got to my new school in Chicago, the students were already doing long division. For whatever reason, no one caught that lapse in my education, and I struggled with mathematics my whole life.

Three years later, at 13, our family picked up once again and continued further west to Southern California. It was a tough summer for me and my sister, because we moved to the San Fernando Valley in early July and didn't attend school until September. Looking back, I'm not quite sure why my parents didn't put us in a summer camp or some type of recreational activity that summer, but they did not.

My sister and I spent that summer playing with each other, watching TV, and missing our friends in Chicago. Perhaps my parents didn't notice our struggle because they were preoccupied during our first few months in California. They were adjusting to living in a new city and state, building a new home, and they had the added burden of having two ill parents who were both hundreds of miles away. Sadly, my mom and dad both lost their mothers by the end of that year. That fall, when I started Jr. High in Southern California, I had the typical fears of making new friends and fitting into a new school. I wasn't a great student, so to compensate, I got involved with social activities in Jr. High and High School. I was a "B" student and never felt compelled to do more than what was expected. Looking back, I know that I had the potential to do so much more, but my parents never taught me the power of intention or focus or how important it was to set a goal. I was not taught personal development or how to become the best version of myself. I don't blame my parents, because they didn't have role models to teach them about mindset, the law of attraction, or "what you think about you bring about." On the contrary, the message I received from my dad was, "if it's not hard, it's not good." My dad learned that mantra from his father. He recounted the story that as a young boy, he had a sledding accident and injured his leg. My grandfather packed the wound with ice and made my dad get back on the sled, teaching my dad the lesson, "if it's not hard, it's not good." This lesson was invaluable to my father as he became a highly successful and well-respected businessman. However, the adage, "if it's not hard, it's not good" did not serve me well, because so many things came easily to me, and I did not feel worthy of the success I was achieving.

Our environment as children impacts who we become in our later years. Our family plays a big role in cultivating our qualities, good and bad. Personal development, positive self-talk, setting goals, and learning to focus on what you want to create are core principles and practices that I live by today. I did not learn these important concepts as a young girl at home or in school. I have a vision that as the world heals from so much adversity and division, the practice of self-love and being good to oneself becomes a concept taught as soon as children begin their schooling.

In High School I found academic studies to be mundane, uninteresting and challenging. I did what I needed to do to walk away from High School with a "B" average and was accepted to the University of California, Santa Barbara.

Looking back, the best education I received in High School was getting involved with Student Government, which had a profound impact in my becoming a successful Network Marketer. That's where I learned about leadership, inspiring others and being an influencer, a cornerstone of success in the Network Marketing industry. Personal Development is a lifelong process. According to Tchiki Davis, Ph.D.

> Personal development can be any skill that you want to develop to improve yourself. But it doesn't really matter which skills you want to improve, the key to personal development is taking the right steps — steps that help ensure that you reach whatever goal you are pursuing.

I believe it is crucial to one's success in any endeavor to embrace these excellent principles and to learn to become the best version of yourself, which is truly a new education.

Meeting fear head-on might be the single greatest challenge in all of life and Network Marketing is no exception. As you begin your new education, know that the growth necessary to achieve success likely means facing down fear.

When I got to college, I felt terribly out of place, whether I was sitting in a large auditorium with over 500 students or a small, intimate class with less than 30 people. Reflecting and pondering why I was miserable in college, I attribute my unhappiness to fear–fear that I wouldn't succeed, fear that I couldn't succeed, and fear that I wouldn't pass any of my exams.

When your desire to succeed becomes stronger than your fear, remarkable things can and will happen in your business and your life. I didn't apply that important lesson when I was in college and that's one of the reasons I dropped out of University after just one semester.

Fear can manifest in many forms. Often people believe that fear of failure and fear of success are the same. I have learned that there is an important distinction between the two. The fear of failure is more about your own expectations of yourself, while the fear of success is more about how others will react to you and what effect that will have on achieving your goals.

Fear of failure (also called "amychophobia") occurs when we allow fear to stop us from doing the things that can move us forward to achieve our goals. You might experience some or all of these symptoms if you have a fear of failure:

- A reluctance to try new things or get involved in challenging projects.
- Self-sabotage - procrastination, excessive anxiety, or a failure to follow through with goals.
- Low self-esteem or self-confidence - commonly using negative statements such as "I'll never be good enough to…." or "I'm not smart enough to ….."
- Perfectionism - a willingness to try only those things that you know you'll finish perfectly and successfully.

Perhaps you have heard the acronym for FEAR = FALSE EVIDENCE APPEARING REAL. When you break down this acronym, it makes perfect sense. The only way you can overcome the fear is to (1) question its validity, (2) ask yourself where that thought came from and (3) have a dialogue with yourself to help you decide whether you want to hold on to that belief (false evidence appearing real) or release it and move forward.

Esther and Jerry Hicks remind us in their book, *The Law of Attraction* that a belief is just a thought that you continue to think.

Back in 1992 when I began my Network Marketing business, I was terrified to reach out to people and to introduce them to my company's products and business. Part of my fear was not knowing what to say, which was a skill I would eventually learn. The other challenge was more deep-seated and a fear that could possibly sabotage the success of my business. It was the fear of what other people would think of me, building "one of those businesses". This was at the forefront of my mind every time I thought of reaching out to someone I knew, particularly since I dropped out of graduate school to pursue a Network Marketing business.

Many people quit their Network Marketing business almost as quickly as they begin because of their concern or fear of what other people think. Lao Tzu, ancient Chinese philosopher said, "Care about what other people think and you will always be their prisoner." The truth is, other people's opinions of us are none of our business. Their opinions have nothing to do with us and everything to do with them.

Most people begin their Network Marketing business to create financial peace and time freedom for themselves and family. If that's the case, then why listen to someone who has no knowledge of this industry and more importantly, is not paying your bills.

My WHY (earning extra money to help with private school tuition) motivated me to overcome the fear of picking up the phone and calling my prospects. Remember **"IF IT'S IMPORTANT YOU WILL FIND A WAY, AND IF NOT, YOU WILL FIND AN EXCUSE."**

I did some research and found a book that not only changed my life but set me on the path to success in my business. It was the first of hundreds of books that I would subsequently read in the personal development arena. *Feel the Fear and Do It Anyway* by Dr. Susan Jeffers was a game changer for me.

I learned from Dr. Susan Jeffers that there are 5 key truths when it comes to fear:

1. **The fear will never go away as long as you continue to grow.** *Every time you take a step into the unknown, you experience fear. There is no point in saying, "When I am no longer afraid, then I will do it". You will be waiting a long time because fear is part of the package.*

   This fear of what other people thought of me was paralyzing. I was petrified to simply pick up the phone and ask one simple question, "would you be willing to try a sample of my product?" I knew it was irrational, but I couldn't bring myself to pick up the phone.

2. **The only way to get rid of the fear of doing something, is to go out and... DO IT!** When you do it often enough, you will no longer be *afraid of that situation. You will have faced the unknown and you will have handled it.*

   So, I had to just DO IT. I had my list; I had the phone numbers (no cell phones back in those days so I had to pick up the phone and call) I had the verbiage from my upline; and I mustered up enough courage to pick up the phone and at least make one call!

3. **The only way to feel better about yourself is to go out and ... DO IT!** *With each little step you take into unknown territory, a pattern of strength develops. You begin feeling stronger and stronger and stronger.*

So, I DID IT! Although my heart was pounding and my hands were sweating, I picked up the phone and dialed and to my great surprise, the first person I called said "Yes". That felt amazing. I survived my first call. So, I picked up the phone and dialed again! To my amazement, everyone who I invited to my very first presentation all said "Yes!"

4. **Not only are you afraid when facing the unknown, so is everyone else.** *This should be a relief; you are not the only one out there feeling fear. Everyone feels fear when taking a step into the unknown. Yes, all of those people who have succeeded in doing what they have wanted to do in life have felt the fear - and did it anyway. So can you!*

   This was a huge lesson for me! In the weeks and months to follow, I picked up the phone and called hundreds of people. And when people said "no" to me, (and they did), I didn't cry, I didn't fall apart, and I didn't give up.

5. **Pushing through fear is less frightening than living with the bigger underlying fear that comes with a feeling of helplessness.** *This is the one truth that some people have difficulty understanding. When you push through the fear, you will feel such a sense of relief as your feeling of helplessness subsides. You will wonder why you did not take action sooner. You will become more and more aware that you can truly handle anything that life hands you.*

   I embraced all the truths that Dr. Jeffers referred to and woke up each day affirming that I was brave, strong, and courageous, even before I picked up the phone. I affirmed, "Reaching out to people about my products is a joyful experience." "Everyone I call is excited to hear from me". "People want what I have." "I am a successful business builder."

I became quite skilled at picking up the phone and even reached out to people whom I considered more prominent and more successful than myself. When I learned to stop caring or worrying about what other people thought of me or my ambition to build a Network Marketing business, my success grew exponentially.

One of my beloved mentors, Rita Davenport was well known for saying, "Don't take advice from anyone more messed up than you!" Here are a few more powerful quotes on caring what others think about you!

"You probably wouldn't worry about what other people think of you, if you could know how seldom they do."

- Olin Miller

"No one can make you feel inferior without your consent."

- Eleanor Roosevelt

And finally Steve Jobs: "Your time is limited, so don't waste it living someone else's life. Don't be trapped by dogma - which is living with the results of other people's thinking. Don't let the noise of other's opinions drown out your own inner voice. And most important, have the courage to follow your heart and intuition. They somehow already know what you truly want to become. Everything else is secondary."

Takeaway Idea

Know Thyself - Grow Thyself.

Take the Action

Having a dialog with yourself can be very powerful. I recommend finding a quiet place where you won't be disturbed, put your pen to paper (or your finger to the keyboard) and ask yourself these questions:

1. What is holding me back from doing the things I need to do to create success?
2. How long will I allow this challenge (these challenges) to continue to hold me back?
3. What is one step I can take immediately to begin to overcome this challenge?

Chapter 10

YOU DECIDE

IS THIS A BUSINESS OR A HOBBY?

I want to share an excellent visual when it comes to our beliefs. Imagine a table. Most Tables have four legs and if one of those legs is wobbly, broken or even missing, the table won't stand. You must have four solid legs for the table to be functional. In Network Marketing you must have a solid belief in four different areas to be successful.

In this chapter we will explore three legs of the table, in other words, three areas of belief: the Network Marketing industry, the Company you have chosen to align yourself with and your company's product or service.

When I first became a distributor, I didn't understand the importance of attending meetings, training, get-togethers, and conferences with my upline and other team members. Within the first two weeks of my becoming a distributor, my upline invited me to a conference in Boston and I honestly thought she was out of her mind. She expected me to leave my husband and daughters for 3 days, spend money, (that I didn't have) fly across the country, stay in a hotel (with someone I didn't know) to attend a national conference. She knew that I could barely afford the starter kit and initial product order, and now, she was encouraging me to spend money just to attend "some conference". Frankly, I was taken aback, disappointed, and even questioned my decision to become a distributor with the company. So, it shouldn't come as a surprise that I declined her invitation and did not attend that conference.

Fast forward, six months later, when my company's semi-annual conference was announced. This event was much closer to my home, and since I had advanced to the first level of the company's success plan, I felt compelled to attend. Two very important things happened at that conference that had a profound impact on the future of my business.

First, I solidified my belief in the Network Marketing Industry. I saw a bigger picture, not only of my company, but also the legitimacy of the Network Marketing Industry. Prior to attending that conference, I felt uneasy, uncomfortable, and even embarrassed telling my "warm market" (my family, friends, and acquaintances) that I was building a Network Marketing business.

I was thrilled to learn that Network Marketing is a brilliant business model and marketing strategy. I left that conference with confidence to share with my family and friends that I had made a smart business decision by choosing to become a Network Marketing professional.

Unfortunately, most of my family and friends were not interested in my business or my company's products. At that point, I was confident enough that I didn't allow their negative attitudes or pessimism to dissuade me in my decision to become a successful Network Marketer. I had no doubt, after attending that conference, that IF I treated my business like a business and not a hobby, it could (and would) completely change the trajectory of my life and the life of my family.

When I attended my first company conference in1993, I wasn't familiar with any statistics regarding Direct Sales or Network Marketing. Here are some statistics that I hope will solidify your confidence that you have chosen to align yourself with an exceptional industry. My hope is that you will feel much more confident than I did 30 years ago.

According to Ventaforce, in 2020 and beyond, the Network Marketing industry is slated to remain one of the highest-earning industries in the global economic diaspora.

Network marketers aren't Amazon, but they have a practical understanding of the new "buy online, at a discount with delivery to the door" phenomenon as local in-store shopping continues to wane. Joining a business built upon this distribution model invites entry into today's world of "working from phone," literally from anywhere there is a wifi connection, and is also excellent preparation for engaging in the future of global commerce.

In 2019, the global network market industry was valued at US $167 billion. Growing diversity in product portfolios and increasing participation of self-employed marketing professionals have driven the industry's growth to date.

As online buying grows, so do estimates of online entrepreneurs. By 2025, the global Network Marketing industry is likely to be worth nearly US $650 billion. It has been forecasted that the Network Marketing industry can witness a year-on-year growth of over 20% in the coming years. With a double-digit CAGR (compound annual growth rate), the Network Marketing industry is expected to surpass a half-a-trillion valuation in five years from now.

Why? According to the DSA (Direct Selling Association) 77% of Americans are interested in flexible, entrepreneurial/ income earning opportunities. Interest is highest among younger online generations, with 91% of "Gen Z"s and 88% of Millennials interested in entrepreneurial opportunities.

Second, I solidified my belief in my company.

Prior to attending that conference, the only people I knew in my company were the person who enrolled me, their upline, and a few other local distributors. At the first national training conference, I had the opportunity to meet many sideline distributors with various educational and ethnic backgrounds as well as different full time and part time careers (many people are growing their Network Marketing business part-time). I was blown away by the culture! I had never been surrounded by so many like-minded people who embraced personal growth and who each shared the same desire to become the best version of themselves. I was fascinated by how everyone I met wanted to support and help each other, which was so different from the typical corporate setting. In a traditional corporate job, many people spend much of their day looking over their shoulders, fearful that their boss is going to discover they are doing something wrong and then, note that discretion in the dreaded personnel file. Even more disheartening, in a traditional corporate setting, there is the fear that a co-worker may stab you in the back and take credit for the work that you did. If that has ever happened to you as it did to me, it is quite painful. Usually, the employee works just hard enough so they don't get fired and the employer pays the employees just enough, so they don't quit. That is not a positive, pleasant work environment.

The other important "ah ha" for me at that first conference was being introduced to the founder and CEO of my company. To see first-hand his vision of the future of our company was truly inspiring. It solidified my belief that I made the right decision to build a Network Marketing business. We were in the corridor of the conference center when my upline looked up and said, "Here comes our CEO; I want to introduce you to him." I was suddenly very nervous, as I had just heard this brilliant visionary address the entire company from the stage. I was floundering, trying to figure out what I would say to this man who seemed larger than life. She addressed him and said, "I'd like you to meet Donna Weiser, who is new to our company and just recently promoted to District Manager" (which was the first rank advancement in my company). He shook my hand and smiled, grinning from ear to ear. I told him I was honored to meet him, and before I could get another word out of my mouth, he said, “So, you’re the hot shot I’ve been hearing all about.” Then it was my turn to smile. I found my words and replied, “I’m thrilled to be part of this amazing company and you’re going to see big things from me very soon, I promise you.” And he did. I didn’t realize it at the time, but when I declared my intention to our Founder and CEO, I was solidifying my goal to achieve great success in my company.

Matthew Wilson is a marketing consultant for organizations and executive teams. Wilson said, “research suggests you are four times more likely to accomplish your goal when accompanied by a public declaration.”

Many goals are private. However, there is something to be said about declaring them. Think about the actions required to achieve your goals; then, choose goals you can declare, and perhaps you will see success achieved more quickly. When I made my declaration to the CEO, do you see how it solidified my belief in my own goal? I had put my commitment out into the universe. How could I fail after committing to him, to me, and to the world that I was going to take this business all the way to the top?

Belief in your company’s product is the third aspect of belief and it’s the easiest of the 4 aspects for several reasons. It’s almost impossible to build a successful Network Marketing business if you’re not madly in love with your company’s product or service. In my experience, a Network Marketing product or service is usually of a higher quality than a comparable brand sold in a retail setting. Why? Because in Network Marketing, we are the advertisers, and we are the brand ambassadors. The money that would normally go to advertisers, (print, TV, or social media ads) and expensive rent in a retail setting can be earmarked for research and development. This allows the Network Marketing Company a competitive edge when it comes to the quality of the product or service.

We are a "word-of-mouth business," literally the most effective market strategy of all. Your mouth is your office. Always keep your office open. Let everyone know how proud you are to represent your company's product or service. And if you are not, perhaps it's time to find another company.

Takeaway Idea

Grab Accountability Partners.

Take the Action

I recommend you share and declare your goals to 3 people in your life who are supportive and want to see you succeed. This will help you articulate your goal as well as create an automatic accountability system for yourself. It also gives you someone to be creative with as you grow and problem solve while pushing you past your comfort zone and your fear.

Chapter 11

LEARNING TO BELIEVE IN YOU

We have explored three legs of the table in the previous chapter. Now comes the fourth and most important "leg", belief in yourself.

Believing in yourself means having faith in your own capabilities. It means believing that you CAN and WILL do anything that it is within your ability. I can almost guarantee that your ability is greater than anything you can even imagine. When you set your mind to do what is necessary you have a much better chance to create success. When you believe in yourself, anything is possible. You can overcome fear, procrastination and self-doubt and have the confidence to take action and make things happen. That is easier said than done.

The opposite of Belief is Doubt. Years ago, one of my peers shared a wonderful visual that clearly demonstrates how just a small bit of doubt can destroy belief.

Imagine two buckets of paint; one filled with white paint and the other with black paint. The white paint represents belief, and the black paint represents doubt. If you took a teaspoon of black paint and mixed it into the bucket of white paint, what would happen? The white paint would become gray. Even just a tiny dropper of black paint will cause the same result, turning the white to gray.

What do these two buckets of paint have to do with our own belief and self-doubt? The white paint represents our belief, and the black paint represents our doubt. We cannot hold on to a belief and a doubt at the same time. So be conscious of your thoughts and resist doubt when it starts creeping in. When we begin with a strong belief in anything, and then allow even a little bit of doubt to creep in, that small amount of doubt is all it takes to tarnish our belief. And sometimes, it's so insidious, we have no idea that it's happening.

Perhaps a comment from a friend or family member causes you to start doubting. You may start to see some success but are haunted by old negative messages. Messages can be deep-rooted and might cause you to feel unworthy of the success you are experiencing. One of the biggest offenders of self-doubt is comparing ourselves to others. The comparison game is as old as humanity, but with the advent of social media, comparing ourselves to others has become a much more serious issue. It can have a profound negative effect on our self-worth and self-esteem.

Here's a great question from zenhabits.net, "If you took the strengths of others, and compared them to your weaknesses, how do you think you'd size up? And do you think this would make you feel good?" Of course not. But that's exactly what we do when we compare ourselves to others, especially on social media. We are only seeing the highlight reels of people's lives on social media, and too often their regrets or disappointments, challenges, or heartaches are omitted. Particularly in the business of Network Marketing, you will seldom, if ever, see a post on social media that says, "10 people said NO to my income option or products today" or "someone quit my team today" or "someone returned all the products they purchased last week." When was the last time you followed someone whose posts portrayed a life filled with sadness or remorse?

My best advice to anyone who continues to compare themselves to others is... DON'T!

Theodore Roosevelt said, “Comparison is the thief of joy.” Let’s heed his powerful words and stop playing the comparison game!

Even before the advent of the internet and social media, I found myself comparing my success to others. The nature of our business is that someone is always dangling a “carrot”, some type of award or reward to motivate you to stretch or push forward. In most Network Marketing companies, once you have reached a milestone or achieved a goal, there’s always something else to strive for. Perhaps it’s a rank advancement, a cash bonus, or a trip to an exotic or amazing destination. Perhaps it’s a car or jewelry. Whatever it is, some people are excited and thrilled at the opportunity to reach for a new goal each month while others find it stressful, paralyzing and debilitating. I believe this is one of the reasons why Network Marketing is not a fit for everyone.

For several years, in the early stages of growing my Network Marketing business, I was frustrated and disappointed in myself; because month after month and year after year, I was unable to achieve the rank advancement goal I had set for myself. What made this situation even more painful and even, oftentimes, unbearable, was the fact that I kept comparing myself to other people who quickly achieved the rank advancement I was hoping to achieve. Each year at our national training conference, I saw these outstanding professionals receive high praise and recognition for achieving their goals. They walked the stage with thousands of people cheering them on. As I smiled on the outside, and cheered and clapped with the masses, I was crying on the inside, questioning my own ability to ever achieve the goal that often felt just out of reach. I doubted my ability as a leader and spent so many hours focusing on what I wasn’t achieving, that I failed to see the many wins that were occurring in my business.

As in any endeavor, these small wins would grow into bigger wins and eventually would support me in achieving major accomplishments that I never, ever dreamed of achieving.

In the course of my studying the concept of "Believe you can succeed, and you will", I came across the story of a woman who exemplifies this philosophy.

Hulda Crooks, who is affectionately known as "Grandma Whitney" successfully scaled Mount Whitney 23 times between the ages of 65 and 91. She climbed 97 other mountain peaks during that time frame as well.

While many people were getting their affairs in order when they approached their 70's or 80's, Hulda, at the age of 91, became the oldest woman to complete the ascent of Mt. Fuji in Japan. How is that even possible?

She had absolutely no doubt that she could continue climbing mountains in her 90's and had a powerfully strong belief in her ability as an athlete as well. Her belief propelled her into the activity that supported the goals she set for herself.

Here is Hulda Crooks describing life at age 80. "Early to bed and early to rise. Out jogging about 5:30 am, jog a mile and walk it back briskly. It takes me 15 minutes to jog a mile and 15 minutes to walk it. Do some upper trunk exercises, work in the yard, walk to the market, and work."

It was a great teaching moment when I learned of this courageous woman's mindset and attitude. If she could have a strong sense of belief in herself and developed the discipline to achieve her goals, then I could certainly revisit my own goals, strengthen my own beliefs, and develop the discipline I needed to create my own success. It also became clear to me, that for several years, the lack of belief in myself, was exactly what was holding me back.

The "Law of Attraction" was one of the most powerful lessons I learned while overcoming my doubt and strengthening my belief. *Ask and It Is Given*, by Esther and Jerry Hicks and *Think and Grow Rich*, by Napoleon Hill, were two of my favorite books that addressed this powerful concept. Simply put, The Law of Attraction states "what we think about, we bring about and what we focus on expands." It's really a simple concept, yet we often complicate it.

Here's an important question. Are you focusing on what you DON'T have in your life or are you focusing on what you would like to attract into your life? When I stopped focusing on lack and focused on prosperity, prosperity came into my life. When I stopped focusing on what wasn't working and I focused on what I wanted to create, amazing things manifested in my life and my business.

How do we change our focus to manifest what we want to create? We start our day with a clear intent on winning the day.

Takeaway Idea
Mind Your Mind.

Take the Action
Put a loose rubber band around your wrist for the next week. Be conscious of what you are focusing on and thinking about throughout the day. When you focus on what you don't have or what's not working, give a gentle snap to the rubber band to remind yourself to be positive and focus on gratitude and the exciting things you are creating in your life.

Chapter 12

WIN THE MORNING, WIN THE DAY

I experienced a huge shift when I embraced the "Law of Attraction" and became acutely aware of how my self-talk was critical for me to create success in my life and my business. The universal law, "The Law of Attraction", is working whether we believe it or not. As Napoleon Hill writes in *Think and Grow Rich*, "Thoughts are things, and powerful at that. Our brains become magnetized with the dominating thoughts which we hold in our minds." Starting off your day with attention to your self talk and mindset can be the difference between a good day and a great day.

I have studied many books and learned from these teachers the importance of winning the day, by winning the morning. Hal Elrod's books *Miracle Morning* and *Miracle Morning for Network Marketers* give explicit instructions on creating a great morning routine.

Hal calls them LIFE SAVERS:

S = Silence (Gratitude, Meditation/Prayer)
A = Affirmations
V = Visualization
E = Exercise
R = Reading
S = Scribbling

Abraham (from the teachings of Abraham Hicks) teaches "If you want to get into alignment with your desires, then the best time to do that is first thing in the morning."

Abraham also teaches us that the morning is one of the most powerful inflection points that determines much of your vibrational range for the day ahead. When you start the day in a good mood, you tend to have a better day, which will reinforce your positive energy. On the other hand, if you don't take the time to consciously raise your vibration and get yourself into a good mood first thing in the morning, there's an excellent chance that stress, obstacles, and other challenges will be your companion throughout the day.

What can you do each day to consciously raise your vibration to begin your day with joy? Meditate first thing in the morning. There are several excellent benefits to meditation, even if you just start with 5 to 10 minutes.

The Mayo Clinic Reports that meditation can give you a sense of calm, peace and balance that may benefit both your emotional well-being and your overall health. And these benefits don't end when your meditation session ends. Meditation can help carry you more calmly throughout your day and may even help you manage symptoms of certain medical conditions.

Deepak Chopra cites the following benefits from meditating.

> **ON THE INSIDE: Stillness, Silence.**
>
> **ON THE OUTSIDE: Boosting immune system, reducing blood pressure and cholesterol, decreasing inflammation, increasing efficiency of oxygen use, reducing anxiety and depression, and increasing telomerase activity. (According to the NIH, the modulation of telomerase activity may have important implications in anti-aging.)**

I spent years complicating the practice of meditation. It's quite simple, but like anything else, thinking about doing something is NOT doing it. Being the perfectionist that I was, doing things perfectly was clearly a hindrance to many areas of my life, including the practice of meditation.

The French philosopher Voltaire said: “Perfect is the enemy of good.”

Perfectionism does have some benefits. For example, it motivates overachievers to pursue their goals; but challenges often occur when perfectionists take things too far, particularly when they set standards that are impossible to meet.

Don’t let perfect become the enemy of the good. A perfectionist will procrastinate because they are afraid of failing before they even begin a task. Procrastination leads to paralysis. Then we end up spending more time thinking about the task than actually doing the task.

Yoda said, “Do or do not. There is no try.” This quote is a simple lesson in commitment and the power in giving something our all, not just giving it a try.

Here’s an exercise. Follow my directions exactly. Place your cell phone down. Now, try to pick it up. Did you pick it up?? If you did, then please put it back down because I did not tell you to pick up your cell phone. I told you to “try” to pick up your cell phone. Put it down again and this time try. Try really hard to pick it up! Did you pick it up? If you did, once again you’re not following my directions. My instructions were to “try” to pick up your phone, NOT, to pick up your phone. This is a perfect example of trying versus doing. Take that word TRY out of your vocabulary. Whatever task you have in front of you, jump in, do the very best you can do to make it happen and celebrate your success. Celebrate the baby steps along the way and celebrate when you complete the task.

Enjoy the journey and it will make completing the task so much sweeter.

Let's dive a little deeper into habits, which will support you in "winning the morning". Are there negative habits that don't serve you, yet you have repeatedly "tried" to overcome these negative habits without success? (There's that word TRY again.) Are there new practices or habits that you would like to embrace?

There are so many great books written on developing new and better habits. The three books that I recommend to support you in developing better habits are Brendon Burchard's *High Performance Habits*, *Atomic Habits*, by James Clear and *The 5 Second Rule* by Mel Robbins.

I learned in *Atomic Habits* to anchor a new habit to an existing behavior. This simple step was life changing for me. The most important part of building a new habit is consistency. Think about a new behavior that you would like to become a habit. Since we are talking about "winning the morning to win the day", identify which behaviors or activities that you do each morning that have already become built in habits. Going to the bathroom, brushing your teeth, taking a shower, or making a cup of tea or coffee, eating your breakfast... These are examples of morning rituals.

Establish New Habits for Growth and Success

Next, identify the new habits you want to embrace and anchor it to an existing behavior. One of the new habits that has improved my life is setting an intention each day before I even get out of bed. I have a recording in my own voice, welcoming me to a new day. One of my mentors, Elly Molina, Intuitive Advisor, helped me solidify this wonderful morning ritual. In my own voice, on a voice recorder I say,

> Good Morning Donna - this is your higher self, waking you up for a beautiful new day. Today, expect miracles. So, repeat after me "'Today, something fabulous is going to

> happen. I don't know what, I don't know when and I don't know how, and I can't wait to find out.'"

Then, I listen to my morning affirmations. My affirmations are so powerful and an important part of my daily morning ritual. They are broken down into 5 areas of my life: physical, happiness, relationships, financial, and general. (See list of affirmations.)

Mel Robbins' *The 5 Second Rule* helped me to win the day when I heard her talk about hitting the snooze button on her alarm clock and how that was disempowering. I certainly related to the challenge of waking up and immediately hitting the snooze button and then going back to sleep. Thanks to *The 5 Second Rule*, I embraced Mel Robbins' brilliant practice of "5-4-3-2-1" and was able to jump out of bed when the alarm clock went off on my cell phone.

I believe those of us who are Network Marketing professionals have an even bigger challenge when it comes to hitting that snooze button because we are our own bosses. When you have a Network Marketing Business you don't have to punch a clock or be expected at a desk at 9 am. When you work from home it's a very short distance from your bed to your desk (which is often the kitchen table). So, what's the big deal if we keep hitting the snooze button?

Actually, it is a big deal, especially if you made an agreement with yourself to wake up at a certain time, and then you don't. Think of it as breaking a contract that you had with yourself.

What happens when you break a promise to yourself? That's exactly what I did every morning when I woke up and looked at my phone instead of beginning my day with gratitude, meditation, prayer, and affirmations.

When you break a promise to yourself, (which is the same as not keeping your word) you chip away at your self worth. If you are continually setting intentions for change or developing new habits, but don't follow through with the behavior change (the new habits), eventually you will lose faith in yourself and your ability to achieve any goal you set. Just as others lose respect for you when you disappoint them by not keeping your word, you will lose respect for yourself, which has its own set of negative consequences.

Stay True to Yourself and Eliminate Distractions

We need to pay as much attention to keeping promises to ourselves as we do to others. Unfortunately, most of us have a historical string of broken promises to ourselves. I will stop smoking. I will lose weight. I will go to the gym to get fit. I will get up early to meditate. The list goes on and on.

When you make a commitment to incorporate new and healthy habits into your routine and you don't follow through, your unconscious mind basically says to yourself, "Yeah right! Good luck with that. You keep saying you are going to do "x y z" and it never happens. Why should this time be different?" This is one of the reasons that we are resistant to declaring our goals.

Each day, when I woke up and immediately checked my messages, I felt frustrated and terribly disappointed in myself. Why? Because I went to sleep the night before and promised myself NOT to look at messages before I did my "miracle morning routine". And all it took was one glance at my phone and I was down that rabbit hole.

It finally occurred to me that my cell phone was a huge contributor to my morning challenge, because my cell phone was my morning alarm.

If your cell phone is your alarm, and you struggle with hitting the snooze button, then move that cell phone across the room, which forces you to get up to turn off the alarm. You can do the same thing if you're using an alarm clock. Remove it from your night table, which forces you to get out of bed to shut off that alarm clock.

I moved my cell phone across the room, which solved the initial challenge of hitting the snooze button when the alarm went off, but I then faced another more insidious dilemma. Checking text messages, email, and social media the moment I shut off the alarm was debilitating. I would be on my phone, checking messages and social media for hours before I even brushed my teeth. Can you relate?

Looking at messages and email the moment you wake up is an unhealthy way to start your day, especially if your intention is to raise your vibration and elevate yourself to a place where the "Law of Attraction" can kick in. I doubt that any of those text messages, Facebook posts or emails will raise your vibration or bring joy to your morning. And it definitely won't support you in starting your day with gratitude.

I spoke to one of my mentors about overcoming this challenge. He suggested that I keep my phone in another room so I wouldn't be tempted to look at it before my morning spiritual practice. Unfortunately, some of the wonderful apps that I use to support my morning practice are phone apps. I solved the problem by getting another phone. One phone is my "personal phone", which has all my apps, podcasts, audio books and voice recorder, (so I can record and listen to my affirmations). I know having two phones may sound a bit extravagant, but this has allowed me to keep my promise to myself NOT to look at social media, text messages or email until I am ready to start my workday.

Setting an intention each morning is another powerful tool to "Win the Day". You can do this by thinking of the things you want to accomplish that day, the outcomes you would like and the people with whom you plan to spend your time. Or you can be more general and state an intention of how you would like to feel that day. The intention I set for myself each morning, whether my day is filled with many activities, or I have an empty calendar, is to have a day filled with joy and happiness and to bring that joy to everyone I see or speak to that day.

Growing in Gratitude

And, last, but certainly not least is to spend a few moments in gratitude. You will have a much more positive day when you consciously think about what you are grateful for, the moment you open your eyes. Or, if you are so inclined, write down at least 5 things for which you are grateful in a gratitude journal.

Research by UC Davis psychologist Robert Emmons, author of *Thanks! How Practicing Gratitude Can Make You Happier*, shows that simply keeping a gratitude journal—regularly writing brief reflections on moments for which we're thankful—can significantly increase well-being and life satisfaction.

When you write down and focus on the things that are already going well for you, you place your attention onto positive energy, which pushes your vibration into a powerful, positive state. By doing this every day, your mind begins to look for the positive experiences that surround you each day, rather than looking at the absence of "that one thing" you really, really want, but don't yet have.

In 1927 at the University of Berlin one of the first great female psychological researchers, Bluma Zeigarnik, was studying human perception in the hope of finding out how the brain decides what to focus on and what to ignore or overlook. She showed many volunteers a circle that was 7/8 complete. Take a moment to look at the shape illustrated here and see what your eyes and your brain tend to focus on.

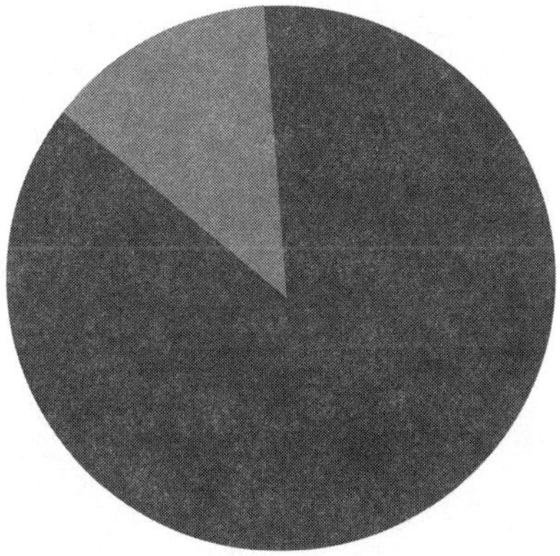

In a series of groundbreaking experiments, she demonstrated that the human brain, which operates like a problem-solving machine, tends to focus more on the unfinished part of the circle. It is as though our brains are programmed to look at the problem, the interruption, or the deficiency and not at what is substantially correct or satisfying.

Researchers call this the "Zeigarnik Effect" and it suggests that we human beings have a problem noticing what's going right in our lives. Our brains long to find something to criticize, something to worry about, or something that's missing or interrupted.

I first learned about the Zeigarnik effect when I read *Seven Prayers That Can Change Your Life* by Leonard Felder. In his first chapter, "A prayer to help you start each morning with a much better frame of mind", Felder says that connecting with God first thing in the morning silently or out loud can make a huge difference in how you will respond to what life presents to you that day. Being human and possessing a problemseeking brain means that at any given moment we are less likely to feel good about our lives and more likely to feel, "no matter what I do is never enough." He says we can outsmart the human brain by beginning each day with gratitude, wholeness, and connection to the miracle of being alive.

Here is an example of my morning routine.

1. The moment my eyes open, I start with a short prayer of gratitude for a new day.
2. Before getting out of bed, I do some simple stretching exercises and listen to my affirmations that are recorded in my voice. By the way, I review and rewrite my affirmations each December when I set my goals for the following year.
3. After going to the bathroom and brushing my teeth, I meditate. DavidJi, one of my meditation teachers, shares a simple technique to help ritualize our morning spiritual practice. His technique is R.P.M. Rise, Pee, Meditate.
4. When it's time to meditate, I will often listen to a brief morning meditation on the app "Insight Timer" that guides me to creating an intention for the day. Or I take 15 to 20 minutes, in silence, following my breath. (Other great free meditation apps are Headspace and Calm)

For many years I only meditated when it was convenient, which wasn't very often. Because it wasn't a priority, I hadn't developed a habit to meditate. Often, weeks, or even months would go by when I did not start my day with meditation. I finally made a conscious decision to make meditation non-negotiable in my life. And now, I love the practice of meditation and can't imagine my life without it.

I have learned that when I do want to make a change in any area of my life, it starts with a thought and then, deciding on what is the next step. Awareness is such a big part of that choice. Often, what we need to do to make positive changes in our lives is right in front of us, but because we are not self-aware, we can't see it. When we take time to shut off the "monkey mind" we can strengthen our awareness. Meditation is an excellent tool to shut off the monkey mind. Monkey mind or mind monkey is a Buddhist term meaning "unsettled or restless".

4 Simple Steps to Mediation

1. Sit or lie comfortably.
2. Close your eyes.
3. Make no effort to control the breath; simply breathe naturally.
4. Focus your attention on the breath and on how the body moves with each inhalation and exhalation.

When you lose focus (and you will) simply go back to focusing on your breath.

Takeaway Idea
Gratitude and good habits can change your life.

Take the Action
If you already have a morning gratitude or spiritual practice, congratulations. I hope you continue to explore and expand your practice to help you become the best version of yourself. If you don't, begin immediately with some type of morning routine to support you in starting your days with appreciation and joy through meditation or starting a gratitude journal.

CONCLUSION

STAYING THE COURSE &
WORKING THE SYSTEM KEEPS YOU MOTIVATED

Over the past 30 years since I became a Network Marketing professional, there have been times when I felt like giving up or quitting, particularly when there were challenges with my company, challenges with my business and challenges in my life. Network Marketing, like any business, has its ups and downs. Those who never quit, persevere and stay the course (as I did) have a much better chance of succeeding than those who start and stop or walk away when it gets challenging.

I have flown across the country to meet a prospect who chose not to meet with me but forgot to tell me. I have driven hundreds of miles to meet with a team member who changed their mind last minute and didn't show up at our appointment and neglected to let me know. I have had leaders at the top rank of my business quit. They walked away because it was too hard, or they couldn't take the rejection or manage the monotony of working the simple business system success requires. I have dear friends and family members who choose not to purchase my products and to this day want nothing to do with my income option.

I love the acronym SW, SW, SW, N. "Some will, some won't so what, Next!" If we continue to plant the seeds, learn to stay out of the results, the seeds will grow. But just like the seeds in a garden, if you don't water them (and nourish them) they won't grow.

I want to remind you, once again, that this is not a "get rich quick" opportunity. It's a "roll up your sleeves and get to work" opportunity. But the good news is, if you roll up your sleeves and get to work, there's a much better chance that you will see success.

Finally, how do we stay motivated, especially during the challenging times? My good friend and mentor, Richard Brooke, is one of the most well-respected Network Marketing professionals in our industry. He built a huge Network Marketing business before he was 30 and owned a very successful Network Marketing company. He is a fabulous coach, author, and speaker. His book, *Mach2 with your Hair on Fire* is a must read for everyone who is interested in "the art of vision and self-motivation". Richard says, "There is a sweet spot of Self-Motivation… It's a place where our bodies, minds and spirits find the most traction to change and produce new results. It's just "beyond boring" and just "short of miraculous".

Start by deciding what you want in life. If Network Marketing is in your future, learn the simple operating system and reach out to those who have gone before you. Believe me, they want to help you. Present your income option and your products or service to others and learn quickly to take yourself out of the outcome - it's not about you. Be gentle with yourself, it's a new venture. As you get into activity, you will grow and learn to manage discouragement and fear and master goal setting and organization. These are all important to any endeavor in life and surely also the keys to success in Network Marketing. Staying the course keeps you motivated and solidifies your belief in our business, our industry and yourself. Grow yourself personally and "mind your mind". It's not an accident that you are reading (or listening) to this book. Remember today more than ever before, people are looking for something. I have spent a wonderful 30 years helping others fit their hopes and dreams into this wonderful "something" called Network Marketing. You deserve success and I look forward to seeing you and your team at the top!

GLOSSARY

MLM - (Multi-Level Marketing, A.K.A Network Marketing) - a legal business model for product and services distribution. For a small sign-up fee, non-salaried consultants or distributors present the company's products and/or services with earnings derived from sales and overrides according to the company's commission system.

Compensation Plans - the compensatory components of commissions, team overrides, and bonuses which may include cars, trips, or other benefits.

Sponsor - the person who recruits you into the business and directs you to training resources.

Upline and Downline - Your sponsor, along with other consultants in levels above you, is considered your "upline." Your upline will receive a percentage of your sales. This will incentivise them to recruit more consultants.

Side line - a team of consultants working under your sponsor but not related to you or your team.

Legs - started by a consultant who recruits other consultants and also builds networks.

Warm Market - people you know and with whom you are acquainted.

Cold Market - people you meet not previously known to you.

LIST OF AFFIRMATIONS

Health

I take care of my emotional, physical and spiritual needs daily.

I am a divinely healthy and fit human being.

I eat foods daily that nourish my body.

I am trim, fit, radiant and vibrant.

I am full of vitality, boundless energy and my body functions perfectly.

I have a strong core and I do exercises daily that strengthen my core & keep me in excellent shape.

Happiness

Life is easy, life is good, life is fun and joyful.

I am deliberately focusing my attention on the positive, the joy, the fun and the incredible.

The feeling of joy, well-being, happiness and success permeates my being every day.

I exude joy and everyone around me feels that and catches it.

I am worthy and deserving of all the wonderful gifts I have and continue to receive.

I have balance and harmony in my life.

Life is fun and life is good. I love this day.

I can't wait to see who shows up in my life today.

Abundance /Wealth

Money flows easily and effortlessly into my life.

I am aligned with the energy of wealth and abundance.

My actions create wealth, prosperity and abundance.

I am a divine magnet for money.

I am open and receptive to all the wealth life offers me.

I always have more than enough.

My wallet and bank balance are overflowing with money.

I create financial abundance so I can give back in amazing ways.

I am a shining example of total prosperity.

I attract all the resources and people necessary to have a prosperous and a wonderful life.

Relationships

My partner (fill in the name) and my relationship is filled with a deep love for each other. It is filled with joy and fun, laughter, romance and passion!

We both strive to be happy and healthy and filled with joy.

We have wonderful goals for the future of our lives that we aspire to achieve together.

I have a great relationship with my family and friends. I see the best in them, always keep them in my prayers and thoughts and focus on their positive qualities.

I only speak kindly of others and I inspire greatness in others.

I strive to be the best I can be and inspire others to do the same.

I am an excellent listener and I am totally present when others are speaking.

FOR FURTHER READING

Ask and It is Given, Esther and Jerry Hicks

Atomic Habits, James Clear

Developing the Leader within You, John Maxwell

Double Your Contacts, Michael Durkin

Feel the Fear and Do It Anyway, Susan Jeffers

GoPro, Eric Worre

High Performance Habits, Brendon Burchard

Mach2 with your Hair on Fire, Richard Brooke

Miracle Morning and Miracle Morning for Network Marketers, Hal Elrod

No Degree Required, Amy Powers

Sacred Powers, Davidji

Thanks! How Practicing Gratitude Can Make You Happier, Robert Emmons

The 5 Second Rule, Mel Robbins

The Four Year Career, Richard Brooke

The Game of Conquering: Strategies To Overcome Fears In Network Marketing, Rob Sperry

The Power of Intention, Wayne Dyer

Think and Grow Rich, Napoleon Hill

What to Say when You Talk to Yourself, Shad Helmstetter